Historic Buildings

HISTORIC BUILDINGS

A Colourmaster publication printed and published by Photo Precision Ltd.
St. Ives, Huntingdon, England.

ACKNOWLEDGEMENTS

The publishers are indebted to the following for permission to reproduce certain illustrations
from their own publications

Miss Patricia Maxwell-Scott (Abbotsford), The Marquess of Exeter (Burghley House), Lady Manvers (Thoresby
Hall), Major Simon Codrington (Dodington House), John Joseph Eyston, Esq. (Mapledurham House), His Grace
the Duke of Marlborough (Blenheim Palace), The Marquess of Bath (Longleat House), David Seton Wills, Esq.
(Littlecote), The Rev. C. E. Harris (Stoke Poges Parish Church), The Rev. C. R. Campling (Pershore Abbey),
The Master, The Lord Leycester Hospital, Warwick,
Nigel Hamilton, Esq. ('Greenwich in Colour', The Greenwich Bookshop, 1971).

FIRST PUBLISHED IN GREAT BRITAIN BY
COLOURMASTER INTERNATIONAL (PHOTO PRECISION LTD.)
ST. IVES, HUNTINGDON, ENGLAND.

ISBN 0 85933 129 6

CONTENTS

Chapter Three
ECCLESIASTICAL

Chapter Four
MISCELLANEOUS

FOREWORD

England, Scotland and Wales harbour such a wealth of old and lovely buildings that the general term 'historic', when it is applied to them, tends often to be employed somewhat lightly. In point of fact, a building is 'historic', rather than 'historical', if it can be connected with specific events, innovations or people of historical significance. Thus in this brief glance at some of the historic buildings of Britain mere antiquity, without additional significance, has by and large been eschewed as a criterion for inclusion.

For the purposes of convenience the selection is divided into four sections: domestic buildings, including stately homes; military structures, meaning castles; ecclesiastical buildings, ranging from fine cathedrals to old and ruined monasteries; and finally a brief survey of some other categories of building that range in scope from university colleges to an old inn.

It would be easily possible to extend the scope to embrace numerous other buildings: St. George's Hospital in London, for instance, which although it no longer exists in its original form is an old-established institution and one with an interesting history in its own right. By the same definition, it would also be allowable to include one of the recent atomic power stations, an early coal mine or even one of the major nineteenth century manufactories. Such an approach would however open numerous floodgates, and by and large all the buildings illustrated in these pages are of interest not only for what they are or have been but also on account of their significance from an antiquarian or architectural standpoint. Taken all in all, the 56 illustrations add up to an architectural panorama of Britain that stands as a reminder of how very rich in such possessions we are.

Chapter One
DOMESTIC

Chatsworth House, 'Palace of the Peak', ancestral home of the Dukes of Devonshire, set amid lovely Derbyshire countryside above the river Derwent, could hardly be bettered as a fine historic residence with which to begin this section. Built in the late seventeenth century in the popular Palladian style of the day, it was the creation of the fourth Earl of Devonshire, later made the first Duke of Devonshire, to recognise the important role he played in securing the English throne for William III.

The first architect, who was responsible for the south and east wings, was William Talman, the King's architect; but the building was completed in 1707 by Thomas Archer, who was responsible for the house's principal feature, its western wing, which in fact constitutes the main front. The Duke spared no expense in erecting his palace, and employed artists and craftsman from all over Europe to carry out the work. Louis Laguerre and Antonio Verrio painted the walls and ceilings, decorative ironwork was provided by Tijou and the fine woodwork was carved by a local craftsman by the name of Samuel Watson; it was this work indeed which so inspired Grinling Gibbons, perhaps the finest wood carver of all time.

The property, as was usual, included its own chapel. Caius Gabriel Cibber was commissioned to design an altarpiece made from Derbyshire alabaster and marble; while within the house itself the Duke set aside a room for a special sculpture gallery, located in the north wing. Among other treasures to be discovered here is Canova's marble of Napoleon's mother. Paintings and other works of art were also imported and among the masterpieces to be inspected at Chatsworth are works by Rembrandt, Van Dyck, Reynolds and many others. There is also an unrivalled selection of old master drawings and in the library is a wonderful collection of rare manuscripts and books.

Chatsworth then is a treasure trove; it is also a wonderful building to behold from the out-side, and the gardens laid out for the sixth Duke by Sir Joseph Paxton (whose great conservatory, now demolished, served as a model for the Crystal Palace of 1851), together with the deer park laid out by 'Capability' Brown during the eighteenth century, are truly picturesque. In the gardens is to be found the Emperor Fountain, whose water rises 290 feet and has a cascade falling 60 feet running down over steps for some 200 yards, before finally sinking into the ground.

These then are a few of the attractions of Chatsworth; if the visitor requires curios he will find them there also, in profusion, not the least of which is the bed in which George II died in 1760, now preserved in a state bedroom and originally presented to the fourth Duke who occupied the position of Lord Chamberlain at the time.

Chatsworth House

This is but one of the fine houses to be found in and around the Peak. Nor is this fact surprising, for the countryside is in truth superb. One other may profitably be considered here and that is **Haddon Hall,** home of the Vernon family since the twelfth century, and of the Manners family, whose head is the Duke of Rutland, since the sixteenth century.

Not a vast palace like Chatsworth, Haddon Hall nevertheless boasts the distinction of being one of the finest medieval houses to be found anywhere in the British Isles. It was built in the main about 1370, and is dominated from the outside by the Great Tower over the main gateway, built by the Sir George Vernon who earned himself the nickname 'King of the Peak'. This leads into a courtyard across which, rising to the full height of the building, is the original Banqueting Hall. Within this is a wonderfully evocative chamber, with its minstrel gallery at one end of the room, fronted by a splendid screen, and the high table at the opposite end, lit by large traceried windows.

In addition to the Banqueting Hall, there is a separate dining room, with a sixteenth century painted ceiling and one of the two large windows lit by heraldic glass. Upstairs there are further fine rooms, including a Long Gallery that measures 110 feet in length, altered and extended during the seventeenth century by Sir John Manners, son of the then Earl of Rutland, and containing wainscoting that some devotees claim is unequalled anywhere.

Adjoining the Long Gallery is an ante-room, the doorway to which has given rise to one of those legends that seem to grow up about every old house. The door is known as Dorothy Vernon's Door, because through it, according to tradition, the only daughter and heiress of Sir George Vernon passed on her way to elope with Sir John Manners and flee with him to the Rutlands' home, Belvoir Castle. Hence the alliance of these two ancient families.

Like all the great houses in this part of Britain, Haddon Hall enjoys the splendid background of the natural terrain hereabouts; but it also has beautiful terraced gardens in its

Haddon Hall

own right, laid out during the seventeenth century and still maintained after the original plans. The entire prospect of this old home, from an architectural and from a scenic point of view, is exceptional, and more than rewarding of a visit.

Passing from one region of great natural beauty to another, **Falkland Palace** in Fifeshire can be singled out for particular mention. This fine old building is unusual in that officially it is still the property of the sovereign, cared for by an hereditary keeper. Although there had been earlier buildings on the same site, the present building dates from the middle of the fifteenth century; it was greatly enlarged about the year 1540 and was used as a hunting palace by several members of the House of Stuart, including James V of Scotland who was responsible for improvements to the property in preparation, it was said, for welcoming his new French bride to the palace. These improvements included the addition of a tennis court.

It was in 1650, when King Charles II was visiting Falkland, that he presented new colours to the troops who had been charged with guarding him; and it is this action that is generally held to mark the origin of the Scots Guards, who as a result retain strong connections with Falkland Palace to this day. Three years after this noteworthy occurrence, in 1653, tragedy in the form of fire descended upon the property: the entire east range of the palace was destroyed. Although Cromwellian troops were encamped nearby at the time, it was not thought that they were responsible for the accident.

After this event the palace was allowed to deteriorate almost to the point of becoming a ruin. It was only in 1855, when the novelist Sir Walter Scott suggested to the then hereditary keeper that he should transform the property into a 'picturesque ruin', that the building received any attention at all, and it was not until 1877 that the decision was taken to undertake a complete renovation of the old palace.

Today Falkland displays much of its original grandeur, while within it has many magnificent attractions, including the King's Room with its large seventeenth century Dutch bed to remind one of its past glory. A fine Chapel Royal has also been preserved, standing as a

Falkland Palace

firm reminder of the palace's Royal pedigree.

Another interesting Scottish residence is **Abbotsford** in Roxburghshire, well known for having been the home of Sir Walter Scott from 1812 until his death in 1832. In addition it is a most attractive border residence, especially notable for its rich decoration and for its works of art.

Scott had always loved the border country, and as soon as his finances enabled him to do so he bought what was then a farm on the banks of the Tweed, together with 110 acres of land, for 4,000 guineas. The property then was known as Cartleyhole, but was given its new name by Scott on account of the land having once belonged to some monks, who had also used a ford close by.

Scott immediately set about formulating plans for enlargement, carried out in 1818; he added a dining room, an armoury and a

Abbotsford, Entrance Hall

conservatory on the ground floor, and further rooms above. Having moved into his new home Scott also set about consolidating his reputation as a novelist by continuing the series of novels now generally known as the *Waverley Novels*, the first of which appeared in 1814.

These novels were an immediate success, and by 1822 Scott was in a position to completely rebuild the old farmhouse, greatly increasing its size. Work was completed in 1824, but even in advance of this, in 1820, the estate had been enlarged to a total of 1,400 acres.

Scott's grandiose notions led to his eventual bankruptcy; but he managed to cling to his beloved Abbotsford, and by the time he died (in his own dining room) he had succeeded, by sheer diligence and application to his writings, in paying off all his debts.

Today Abbotsford stands as a monument to Scott, and as a reminder of the many famous men and women who visited him there, ranging from Wordsworth to Washington Irving. It is open to members of the public, and among other attractions is the study in which Scott conceived and wrote his well loved novels.

Passing from Scotland to the less savage terrain of Northamptonshire one finds several fine residences. Conspicuous among them is **Burghley House,** just south of Stamford, built by that William Cecil who became Elizabeth I's favourite and was created first Lord Burghley.

Here is a truly magnificent structure, erected between 1577 and 1587 and standing on the site of an older manor which Burghley pulled down to make room for it, curiously enough also, in earlier times, the site of a monastic cell. Burghley House is held by many to be the finest

Elizabethan mansion in Great Britain; it is certainly the largest, with its 145 rooms; it is also one of the wealthiest in terms of art treasures, with paintings by such masters as Holbein, Velasquez, Michelangelo, Van Dyck, Rembrandt, Titian and scores of others.

Burghley's expressed purpose in creating this vast palace was to provide lodging for his Queen whenever she should decide to pay him a visit, and it must have come as something of a disappointment to the powerful nobleman that she actually only stayed here on twelve occasions. As though to offset this fact there is today at Burghley House a carefully preserved Queen Elizabeth Room.

Other notable rooms include a Purple Satin Bedroom hung with Mortlake Tapestries, a Pagoda Room which has forty portraits about its walls and whose principal decoration is a mother-of-pearl model of a Chinese pagoda, and finally a Billiards Room, with a billiards table manufactured from oak taken off the *Royal George* wrecked off the Isle of Wight in 1782.

Burghley House was designed by John Thorpe, and his plans for the structure are preserved today in the Soane Museum in London. As with similar buildings, he graced it with a private chapel, with wall carvings by Grinling Gibbons. They do not represent Gibbons' finest work, but they are of great beauty nonetheless, and well reward inspection.

It is an interesting fact that one of the most sumptuous of all stately homes to be built or rebuilt during the nineteenth century, **Thoresby Hall,** in Nottinghamshire, home of the Pierrepont family, can be associated in some slight way with the magnificence of Burghley House: for the architect, Anthony Salvin, who had been responsible for the restoration of Windsor Castle, based the entrance tower on that at Burghley House. He built the imperious

Burghley House

Thoresby Hall, Great Hall

Thoresby Hall over the years 1864-71.

The present structure is not the first great house to have stood on this site, and indeed its predecessor was only taken down at the instigation of the third Earl Manvers because he thought it stood too close to the lake and was therefore subject to damp, as well as being too small for his requirements.

The Pierrepont family can trace its English ancestry back to 1066 when Robert de Pierrepont accompanied William on his invasion of Britain. Thereafter the family established itself as a powerful and constantly active force in the affairs of the realm, until in the reign of Elizabeth I Sir George Pierrepont could claim ownership of a total of nine manor houses.

Sir George's grandson was created Earl of Kingston in 1628, and then in 1715 the fifth Earl was created Duke of Kingston-upon-Hull. It was William, the fourth Earl, who initiated the building of the first house at Thoresby in 1683. The architect was William Talman, subsequently builder of Chatsworth House; he employed Caius Gabriel Cibber as sculptor.

This house survived until 1745, when it was destroyed by fire; it was replaced four years later by a building designed by John Carr, then the best known architect in the north of England. This was the house that came into the possession of the second and last Duke, Evelyn Pierrepont, who succeeded to the title at the age of fifteen and died without an heir in 1773.

It was then that the house passed to his elder

sister's son, Charles Meadows, who assumed the Pierrepont name and became Earl Manvers in 1808. It was his grandson who was responsible for the present structure; and although it can be condemned for having supplanted an attractive eighteenth century residence it has to be admitted that it is a highly successful creation.

The architect Salvin was an authority on medieval and Tudor architecture, and incorporated his observations into this house. Most successful of all the chambers, perhaps, is the Great Hall, some 64 feet long, 31 feet in width and an awe-inspiring 50 feet in height, rising up through three storeys, panelled with white and red oak from Sherwood Forest and decorated with armour, weapons and family portraits.

There are other impressive features; but the overall effect is of a very successful attempt at a grand residence, created in an age one would not normally associate with such structures.

A complete contrast to the two preceding houses is to be found in **Moreton Old Hall** in Cheshire, one of the most unusual, as well as most lovely in appearance, of all domestic buildings included here. The slightly warped appearance it has today, brought about by the passage of time, has only added to its picturesqueness.

This marvellous relic of black and white craftsmanship was first projected about the year 1520, but was added to later in the sixteenth century. It is sometimes called Little Moreton Hall to distinguish it from Great Moreton Hall, a building which no longer exists in its original condition, and was built first of all in the shape of a letter 'H', with a Great Hall forming the central feature, the lord's chambers placed at one end and the kitchens at the other. The later additions altered this shape significantly, until it became virtually a quadrangle. These included the gatehouse, a porch over the entrance to the Great Hall and the two famous hexagonal bay windows with their inscriptions to the effect that they were made 'by the grac of god' by one Richard Dale in the year 1559.

If the exterior of Moreton Old Hall is of singular appearance the interior too contains several particular features. There is for instance a wonderful kitchen range, perfectly preserved, with an open fireplace that measures eleven feet in width and five feet in depth. In the west part of the house there are two secret rooms, entered through sliding panels. Then on the third floor there is a magnificent ballroom measuring some 75 feet by twelve, together with a retiring room.

These are but a few of the attributes of this fine old building; but surely its greatest wonder is its external appearance, richly reflected in the surviving moat and a positive feast of decorative craftsmanship.

Another fine Tudor house, but of a completely different character, is **Compton Wynyates** in Warwickshire, dating from the latter part of the fifteenth century but standing on the site of a much earlier building that had been the property of the Compton family as early as the thirteenth century. The present house was begun about 1481 by Edmund Compton and completed about 1515 by his

Moreton Old Hall

15

son, Sir William Compton, in which year the chapel was added.

Sir William Compton was one of Henry VIII's favourites, and frequently the monarch stayed at Compton Wynyates; so too did later English monarchs, including Elizabeth I, James I and Charles I. Their monograms are still to be inspected on the plaster ceiling of what is known as Henry VIII's Room.

The Comptons later became Earls of Northampton, and it was under this title that the family became staunchly Royalist during the Civil War, surrendering their lovely house to the Cromwellian forces in 1644, following a two day siege. Justly proud of the building, the Comptons did not risk its destruction by attempting to recapture it; instead they took up residence at another family house, Castle Ashby, where they continued to spend most of their time following the restoration of the monarchy. They retrieved Compton Wynyates

in 1646 for the sum of £20,000. Because of this the house is today very little altered from its original construction, only some nineteenth century Gothic windows standing as testimony to later additions.

The exterior of this fine building is characterised by the bristling array of twisted chimneys that seem to spring from all parts of the roof. The house is set in lovely gardens, particularly noted for their shrubbery and hedges, trimmed into a variety of decorative shapes.

Inside there is also much to admire, including plaster ceilings and wood panelled walls, as well as much furniture dating from the house's earliest days. The original chapel has not, alas, survived, being replaced by a new building about 1665.

Moving over to the west country, to Gloucestershire, **Dodington House** and park demand inclusion in these pages. The present

Compton Wynyates

16

Dodington House, West Front

house dates from 1797, designed by James Wyatt at the instigation of its owner, Christopher Bethell Codrington, whose descendants live in the house still.

The 1797 building was really no more than an ambitious extension to an older, Elizabethan manor house, and took some twenty years to complete. This earlier building had been erected about 1560 for one Thomas Weekes; but even before that time there had been a manor house on the site. It was soon after completion of this Tudor building that Dodington passed into the hands of Giles Codrington.

Over the years various members of this family have achieved a great deal; but surely the most eminent of all was that Christopher Codrington after whom the famous old library at All Souls College, Oxford, is named, and who bequeathed £10,000, together with his own collection of books, to found the library. Another famous son was Admiral Sir Edward Codrington who successfully commanded H.M.S. *Orion* at Trafalgar.

The house in its present form is a first class example of the neo-classical style favoured during the eighteenth century, with lovely grounds and lakes laid out by 'Capability' Brown. Dodington is generally considered to be one of Wyatt's most successful designs. He unfortunately perished in an accident while the the house was still under construction, in 1813, when he and his employer were travelling in a coach. Avoiding a collision with a post chaise, the coach overturned and poor Wyatt was killed instantly. The large hexastyle portico on Corinthian columns that crowns the west front of this fine residence must be regarded as his major contribution to the house's exterior; it is of sufficiently large dimensions to allow carriages to drive right up to the front door.

Within, too, the house is conceived on a grand and luxurious scale. The principal

17

feature, to be observed immediately after passing from the Entrance Hall, is the fine staircase and staircase hall, the hall itself rising the entire height of the building and possessing both upper and lower galleries, with stairs branching into two separate flights, apparently unsupported and lending the whole a most attractive lightness of appearance. Throughout the house, which is open to the public, this same graciousness is in evidence.

A number of fine houses have been erected over the years close to the banks of the Thames, flowing through Berkshire and Oxfordshire; and not surprisingly, for this is delightful country. One such residence, the historic home of the Blount family, is **Mapledurham House** in Oxfordshire, begun in 1588 by Sir Michael Blount, Sheriff of Buckinghamshire and later of Oxfordshire, later also Lieutenant of the Tower, charged with keeping surveillance over

Philip, Earl of Arundel, among other notorious prisoners.

The Blounts are descended from the Le Blonds, who settled in England soon after the Conquest. Their house is a fine Tudor structure, exemplifying the best qualities of a medium-sized country residence of that time, packed with mementos in the form of family portraits of earlier Blounts—of Sir Charles Blount, for instance, who was killed in the Battle of Oxford supporting the King, a soldier and scholar who added many fine books to the library at Mapledurham. His portrait by W. Dobson stands in the Entrance Hall, in itself an unusual room on account of the walls being panelled in light oak on their lower portions only.

The house is built of red brick. The name of its architect, as well as that of the gardener responsible for the lovely grounds, is unknown.

Mapledurham House

The house was completed during the early seventeenth century, and with the exception of the castellations on the front parapet—added during the Civil War—and the porch, it stands exactly as it did when new.

Within there are numerous apartments worthy of inspection: the Library stocked with rare old tomes, the Saloon, the Dining Room, whose walls are painted a delicate lime green, and many others. There is also a fine collection of paintings displayed throughout the house, including a first class portrait of the poet Alexander Pope by Godfrey Kneller.

The Blounts were always a strong Roman Catholic family; among the many interesting chambers at Mapledurham is an exquisite little private chapel, built in 1789 just before the French Revolution, at a time when English Catholics were contending with severe recriminations. Permission had to be obtained to build this chapel, a proviso being made that the exterior must not resemble a religious building, whatever the interior looked like.

All in all Mapledurham is a delightful house. It is however dwarfed and surpassed in its popular appeal in Oxfordshire by the magnificence of **Blenheim Palace,** home of the Dukes of Marlborough and birthplace of Sir Winston Churchill.

The palace emerged directly from the victory at Blenheim, on August 13, 1704, of John Churchill, first Duke of Marlborough, over the French. His victory was decisive, and it was followed by others. Parliament considered it so auspicious that, at the instigation of Queen Anne, it voted £500,000 to build this palace for the general.

That Marlborough enjoyed the Queen's favour in this instance, as also in his obtaining a Dukedom somewhat earlier, is usually

Blenheim Palace, South Front

attributed to the influence of his wife. It was the Duchess also who rejected the plans for Blenheim submitted by Sir Christopher Wren, choosing those of Sir John Vanbrugh instead.

The foundation stone was laid in 1705; the building, covering an area of some three acres, was completed in 1722. The park, covering some 2,500 acres, was conceived in the first place by Henry Wise, the Queen's gardener; it was modified at a slightly later date by 'Capability' Brown. The park and gardens are indeed one of Blenheim's most magnificent properties, the most splendid feature of all perhaps being the Triumphal Way, designed by Sir William Chambers.

The architecture of the house is of extreme splendour, Vanbrugh's own personality by no means submerged by the immensity of the project. It is built around three sides of a large courtyard, in two storeys. The large central wing is graced with four turrets and an impressive portico set on Corinthian columns. The two side wings are connected to the main block by means of colonnades of Doric columns. Within this ducal palace is housed a collection of works of art and furnishings that are bound to impress every visitor to Blenheim.

It is impossible to list all the palace's wonders; they include magnificent state rooms, carvings by Grinling Gibbons, a painted ceiling by Sir James Thornhill recording the Battle of Blenheim and, most impressive of all, the tapestries manufactured in Brussels depicting the various military achievements of the Duke of Marlborough.

Here indeed is a palace to compare with any in Europe, a magnificent testimonial of the gratitude of the English nation to one of its pre-eminent military leaders.

In Wiltshire there stands another magnificent residence, this time the home of the Marquess of Bath, **Longleat House,** a fine Elizabethan structure that has survived the centuries virtually intact (see page 8).

Originally Longleat was a monastery, a thirteenth century Augustinian foundation. Like all other such establishments, it was dissolved by Henry VIII and passed into the hands of the Crown, being sold in 1540 to Sir John Thynne. He began building his new home in 1547, but unfortunately much of what he accomplished perished by fire in 1567 and building began for the second time the following year, virtual completion being effected by the year of Sir John's death, 1580.

No record is preserved of an architect's name, and it is assumed that Thynne himself was responsible for the overall design of his house, importing his building materials from many parts of Britain, including a quarry at Haslebury near Bath which he bought especially for the purpose. The present park is a later creation, that of the unwearying 'Capability' Brown, laid out between 1757 and 1762.

The inside of this lovely building accords perfectly with the impressive exterior. Its treasures are myriad and its furnishings and decorations quite superb. The Great Hall, with a minstrel gallery added about 1660 and an ornate fireplace added at a later date, is otherwise as Sir John Thynne conceived it, with a stone-flagged floor and hammer-beam ceiling supports. It is basically a large, open, slightly austere chamber; other apartments are far more elaborately conceived.

They range from the wonderful 'Red Library'—so called because of the colour of the walls—where only a small part of the large collection of books at Longleat is housed, to the magnificent State Dining Room, its walls covered with tooled Spanish leather dating from 1620. It was here that Queen Elizabeth dined as the guest of Sir John Thynne, before the house was completed, and many other Royal and distinguished guests have dined in it.

The longest room in the house is the Saloon, some 90 feet in length and in Elizabethan times known as the Long Gallery. It is decorated with sixteenth century Flemish and French tapestries. Other art treasures at Longleat include paintings by Titian and Van Dyck, not to mention a magnificent painted ceiling in the State Drawing Room, adapted from one in the library of St. Mark's Cathedral in Venice. Among the curios in this room is a writing table that once belonged to Talleyrand.

A second house in Wiltshire worthy of attention is **Littlecote,** a Tudor manor house dating from 1490-1520, although an earlier house stood close by as early as 1200, remains of which can still be seen.

Littlecote, Great Hall

Littlecote lies beside the Kennet, and in the thirteenth century belonged to one Roger de Calston. It came into the possession of the Darrell family in 1415, when Elizabeth de Calston married William Darrell. The Darrells retained the property until 1589, when it passed into the hands of Sir John Popham, Lord Chief Justice of England, whose family owned the house until 1922. In that year Sir Ernest Salter Wills came to live at Littlecote, and he it was who restored it to its present immaculate condition.

Its treasures are numerous. In the Great Hall there is a fine Elizabethan screen, and stained glass in the south windows dating from the early sixteenth century, probably Flemish in origin. In the Dutch Parlour, so called because some of the paintings about its walls are supposed to have been painted by Dutch prisoners of war, there are paintings covering the entire room, including a panel showing scenes from *Don Quixote* along one wall and Justice and Fame supporting the Popham Arms on the ceiling. There is a William of Orange Bedroom, where Prince William slept

in 1688 and which contains one of a probable set of sixteen Brussels tapestries made for the Prince between 1675 and 1700, this one depicting Hercules and Apollo supporting his arms as King of England

These are a few of the attractions; there are also a Queen Elizabeth I Bedroom, a Long Gallery and the Great Hall, all of them commanding attention and all of them illustrating the sturdy Tudor magnificence of Littlecote to fine advantage. There is a collection of Cromwellian armour and weaponry in the Great Hall that is unique. There is also a so-called 'Brick Hall'—a name deriving from its having a brick floor—with wonderfully darkened seventeenth century panelling, together with furniture of a similar date. The painting over the fireplace in this room is of Charles, Duc de Bourbon, painted by Sebastiano del Piombo, and a major attraction.

Lastly a Royal residence, though it is not one any longer; a residence, moreover, that might be regarded as one of the most monumental follies of all time. This is **The Royal Pavilion** in Brighton, built for George IV while he was still

21

Royal Pavilion, Brighton

Prince of Wales in 1787. The architect was Henry Holland and the Saloon is the principal part of his structure, its ceiling painted to resemble the sky, its walls covered in rich yellow Chinese wallpaper. Another room of the same era is that known as 'Mrs. Fitzherbert's Drawing Room', furnished with a suite of lovely Sheraton satinwood furniture originally belonging to the actress and taken from her Brighton home.

It was in 1815 though that the Royal Pavilion acquired the personality that is today most associated with it, when John Nash made certain additions, including the famous Banqueting Room with its great domed ceiling painted to resemble a palm tree. In the branches of this palm a great silver dragon holds an immense chandelier like a cascade of diamonds, out of which rise five smaller dragons carrying lotus shaped lights.

Nash also added the Music Room, decorated in the Chinese style that was the fashion of the day, the walls painted with red and yellow lacquer and gold; it also has lotus shaped lights set in decorative chandeliers, and above all it has a domed ceiling formed of innumerable gilded scallop shells.

As well as these rooms there are the King's private apartments, situated on the ground floor. Like all other parts of the interior of this sumptuous residence they evoke images of the flamboyant period of the Regency when extravagant merry-makings were the order of the day and night with the Prince Regent and his circle. Nor does the outside of this fabulous building fall short of them in its Oriental copyings, its domes and splendid gardens. It is true that the North Gate was not part of the original plan and was added by William IV in 1832, and that the South Gate was set in place as late as 1921, a gift from the people of India, but even so the immediate visual impact of the Royal Pavilion carries one easily back to the elegant days of the early Georges.

Brighton was then the most fashionable seaside resort in southern England, and there is still much that savours of these times; into this setting the Royal Pavilion fits perfectly, having on public display a permanent collection of furniture, carpets, silver and numerous other treasures.

22

Chapter Two
MILITARY

The castles of England, Scotland and Wales display between them a wide variety of functional and architectural traits; they were built at different times, and they were built for different reasons. One thing is certain, and it is that the Normans were the great castle builders, strengthening their military and strategic positions following the Conquest of 1066.

Among all the castles for which they were responsible none has remained in such an impressive state of repair as that at **Alnwick,** in the extreme north of England in Northumberland, one of a chain of castles to the south of the English-Scottish border calculated to defend the conquerors against the Scots. This pre-eminent castle in the chain has been the home of the fighting Percys, whose head is the Duke of Northumberland, ever since it was first built some seven centuries ago. It is still lived in by the family, the expansive fortress totally dominating the town which has grown up about it; and considering the violence it has witnessed over the centuries its survival is a matter for congratulation.

The Normans built only wooden palisades about their strongholds, but these they graced with stone gatehouses in the form of small towers. At Alnwick the original gatehouse is still to be seen, though strengthened from the fifteenth century onwards by the addition of two square turreted towers, behind which are a further two octagonal towers. Placed atop these towers are the defiant figures carved in stone of what are supposedly sentries calculated to ward off prospective trespassers. Between the two pairs of towers once ran the moat, traversed by a drawbridge.

The main block of the castle complex lies securely beyond this. Here are the keep and its

Alnwick Castle

surrounding defences, the chapel, guard chamber and other domestic chambers, all built around an inner bailey, or courtyard, scene of many a violent and unpalatable deed in past years but now given over to more sedate ways. The entire castle area covers a large expanse of ground, embraced by what are called curtain walls, interrupted by several towers all with individual names and purposes—such as the Falconer's Tower and the Warder's Tower—erected during the fourteenth century. The overall impression is of complete invincibility, and one is left in no doubt as to why this most precariously positioned of all English military structures should have survived.

South of Alnwick is another great Norman bastion, **Richmond Castle,** one that has survived only as a ruin. Perhaps because of this, however, it has over the years been surrounded by unfounded legends: that King

Richmond Castle

Arthur and his Knights of the Round Table sleep beneath the stones of the keep, for instance, or that the so-called Gold Hold Tower, one of those set about the majestic curtain walls that are the castle's chief glory, has a treasure trove of gold buried beneath its foundations awaiting the fortunate discoverer. Its situation high above the Swale only adds to the romantic aura that surrounds this fine old eleventh century structure.

Richmond was the Conqueror's gift to Alan Rufus, who had fought beside him in the invasion. He was created first Earl of Richmond, and immediately set about establishing his stronghold in this northerly situation. His first defences were of wood and earth, but having once established himself and surrounded his fortress by strong stone walls he immediately began to replace wood by stone elsewhere, concentrating first of all on the magnificent 100 foot high keep, with walls that are in places eleven feet thick.

Even more impressive are the high stone curtain walls that surround the fortress. Richmond was in point of fact one of the first castles in England to boast walls of stone rather than the customary wooden palisades. Since the keep had not been built at the time of their erection an entrance way was cut straight through the walls, and then the keep placed above it, incorporating some of the finest Norman masonry in the country. Among the other towers placed about the walls is one called the Lion Tower, so named because William the Lion, King of Scotland, was imprisoned in it after his defeat at the Battle of Alnwick in 1174, a clear illustration of why it was so necessary to have these northerly strongholds.

But it was not simply the Scottish border that had to be guarded; the Welsh border too had to be held, and along it, on either side of the ancient Offa's Dike, was established a chain of castles, among which to the north was **Ludlow,** erected towards the close of the eleventh century by Roger de Lacy, in the form first of all of the large keep which is known today as the Great Tower.

Curtain walls, both inner and outer, with further defensive towers, were added immed-

Ludlow Castle

iately afterwards; thereafter additions were made as and when they were thought necessary. These features testify to the fact that in its early days Ludlow was highly important for defensive purposes; from the north the castle was virtually unassailable, the river Teme flowing amiably far beneath it. Later its military importance diminished; the Welsh no longer needed keeping at bay. Its inhabitants therefore concentrated on making it a gracious place in which to live, not a forbidding fortress. Its high point, at least from a literary person's point of view, was the first performance in its Council Room in 1634 of John Milton's masque · of *Comus*, an entertainment—one of many given there—combining both words and music in mainly processional form. Only the Civil War roused the fortress from its old somnolence, for then Ludlow was a Royalist stronghold and among the very last towns to surrender to the Parliamentarians.

Over the ensuing years Ludlow Castle was allowed to crumble, so that what remains today is to a large extent ruin, though still substantial, and marvellously evocative of the past. There is Mortimer's Tower, a Hanging Tower, a little circular Norman chapel in the inner bailey and many other features. Ludlow itself is a lovely town, full of ancient buildings, and the unimpassioned grandeur of this old fortress accords with it admirably.

Similarly **Chepstow,** site of the southernmost castle in this chain, and doubly important

Chepstow Castle

strategically because of that. This castle was begun in 1067 by William FitzOsbern, another follower of William the Conqueror, one of the very first castles to be conceived following the invasion of 1066. Once again it was the keep that received precedence when building got under way, and this dates from the eleventh century; but much of the present ruins date from the thirteenth century when Roger Bigod, fifth Earl of Norfolk, partly rebuilt and considerably expanded the structure.

Bigod's extension consisted of a series of courts following the contours of the cliff upon which Chepstow Castle is perched, high above the river Wye, while the four courtyards are overlooked by the hall-keep, which stands some 40 feet high. The thick curtain walls are broken by round towers, and massive gatehouses stand at both entrances to the castle. Among other notable features is the

tower known as Martin's Tower, for some twenty years the prison of the regicide of that name (he died in 1680 and is buried in Chepstow church). Another famous prisoner kept within the castle walls was Jeremy Taylor, confined here in 1656.

Another prominent castle to have grown up as a result of the Norman occupation was of course that at **Dover,** and of all English castles there is perhaps none as capable of invoking feelings of patriotism as this. It dates back to a time long before the Conquest and it is estimated to be some 900 years in age; it was here, in 1066, that King Harold finally surrendered to William of Normandy.

During pre-Norman times Dover Castle was not of course a castle as one thinks of such buildings now; it was rather an earthen structure, settled on an eminence and selected precisely because it commanded a view right

26

across the English Channel, also because it was virtually unassailable from the land. Immediately following the invasion the Normans set about erecting the first portions of the castle as it survives today; refinement continued century by century as the demand continued for ever stronger battlements about what was called the 'Key of England'. It was during the twelfth century that the castle's outstanding feature was added in the form of a colossal keep, its entrance dominated by two enormous towers with further bastions beyond them.

It was Henry II who began the practice of gracing his castles with these huge keeps; he considered them of paramount importance in the defence of his military establishments. For some reason, and it may have been because Henry died before that at Dover could be completed, the keep was never finished; but it remains today in good repair at the heart of a vast complex of inner and outer walls with aptly named towers and gates set at intervals about them. Most notable of all is the Constable's Gate, a massive arched gateway set between drum-towers. The Constable was the governor or warden of the castle, and so important a position did William the Conqueror hold this to be that he placed his own half-brother, Odo of Bayeux, in it. Later honorary holders of the office have included both the Duke of Wellington and Sir Winston Churchill.

Dover Castle

Further west but also important in the southern defences of the realm lies **Carisbrooke Castle** on the Isle of Wight, an establishment that boasts more antique origins than those even of Dover, for a part of the stonework of the early castle dates back to Roman times.

Today Carisbrooke is the home of the Governor of the Isle of Wight—at present Earl Mountbatten of Burma—as well as being a museum. Prior to that it was the residence first of all of the Lords of the island and then of the Captains. Its historical significance stems both from its architectural interest and from the events with which it has been connected, most notable of all being the imprisonment of Charles I, who was kept here for almost a year and who tried in vain to escape.

The futility of his attempt is not to be wondered at, for Carisbrooke is strongly fortified, having been strengthened several times over the centuries. The bulk of the foundations date back to Norman times, with such later additions as fourteenth century drum towers enclosing the main gateway and sixteenth century rampart walks and artillery bases that were added at the express command of Queen Elizabeth I.

The central keeps of Norman castles were constructed from earth, piled high on the ground, tightly enclosed by wood and then built on, again with wood. During the twelfth century, as at Dover, the earthenwork keeps were replaced in newer buildings by sturdy stone keeps which had the the great advantage of being less prone to fire damage. Possessors of castles that boasted only the old-fashioned earth and wood mottes quickly hit upon the idea of encasing them in stone, and these

Carisbrooke Castle

28

Newark Castle

became known as shell-keeps. That at
Carisbrooke is generally held to be one of the
best examples, and one has to climb a flight of
over sixty steps before entering it.

This is but one of the features worthy of
attention. Other attractions include fifteenth
century doors, the Great Hall, St. Peter's
Chapel (with its leper squint in the south wall)
and a well with an ancient tread wheel.

Among other fine English castles **Newark**
claims attention, for there is something
unusually decorative about this East Midlands
fortress set in the middle of an old market town
that would seem to have no particular
eminence or other natural feature to lend it
strategic value. The original ownership of the
castle is also out of the ordinary. It was an
ecclesiastical property, inhabited by the Bishop
of Lincoln who was also Lord of the Manor of
Newark.

The original structure was of wood,
completely replaced by stone in 1175. The
domestic appearance of the outer walls is
explained by the Great Hall being erected not,
as was often the case, in the main yard of the
castle but actually on the scarp of the
ramparts, with a basement tunnelled out
beneath it.

It was in 1216 that King John died in
Newark Castle, and it was two years later, in
1218, that the fortress withstood its most
ferocious siege. Thereafter peace came to the
castle, and then for the second time it
was given over to clerical inhabitants.
Throughout the greater part of the thirteenth
century and the early part of the fourteenth a
total of some nine bishops were in residence
here. It was during their occupancy that the
decorative elements were added to the exterior,
most markedly about the windows, particularly

Tintagel Castle

the large bay or oriel window, so positioned to allow a maximum light to fall on the lord's high table which was set on a dais in the Great Hall.

Because peace came to Newark the history of its castle became unspectacular; the Civil War, during which the town observed Royalist sympathies, naturally brought new violence down upon the castle. During these troubled times it underwent the fierce siege that left it in the derelict condition in which it may be observed today, the river Trent flowing calmly by beneath its walls.

All of those castles so far described have survived at least to the extent of being substantial ruins, but there are many others that have not done so. None is more representative of this category perhaps than **Tintagel Castle** in Cornwall, consisting really of very little more than an outline of a castle on the rocky coast above an angry ocean.

But if little of the building to speak of remains at Tintagel a good deal remains in the way of legend, legend moreover that has become a part of traditional English folklore, even if it is unsubstantiable and almost certainly bogus: for Tintagel probably never was an Arthurian stronghold, and it may well be that Sir Tristram never did woo Isolde within its walls. Cadbury Camp, near Glastonbury, may have been the legendary Arthurian fortress; Tintagel was not.

Even so, the romantic aura of the few remaining ruins serves to draw the tourists here each year. The ruins they find actually date from the first part of the twelfth century when Roger, first Earl of Cornwall and son of Henry I, began to build his fortress on this site. Little remains, though parts of a later, thirteenth century wall are still observable, together with some 90 feet of the structure of the Great Hall which they enclosed. In all probability this hall was a magnificent structure, though there is now no way of determining how it may have looked in all its glory.

The fortress did not long survive, being allowed to fall into disrepair under heavy sea winds. Its one period of somewhat questionable significance came during the fourteenth century when it was utilised as a prison. And so perhaps it is pleasant still to think of Tintagel in Arthurian terms, or at any rate Celtic terms: for it has been discovered that long before the first Earl of Cornwall came to this spot it was the home of Celtic monks, a few of whose ancient rock-cut graves are still preserved.

Further east, this time on the south coast in Dorset, lies **Corfe Castle.** At the time of its strategic significance Corfe was the most important castle in Dorset, set proudly on the Purbeck Downs; now it is a sorry ruin, reduced by the Parliamentarians during the Civil War after a prolonged siege which was stoutly defended by Lady Bankes.

Before the castle was built, during the twelfth century, there stood on the site it now occupies a hunting lodge in which Edward the Martyr met his death by assassination in 979. The Norman structure was placed on a comparatively narrow piece of high ground, and because of this it assumed a very roughly triangular configuration. Both the outer and middle gates possessed drawbridges and had two flanking towers, while access to the inner bailey and the castle proper was through a narrow inner gate. The imposing Buatavant Tower guarded the north and west sides of the inner bailey, and was itself protected at its entrance by a portcullis and forebuilding. Today it is still possible to follow the full design of the castle and to appreciate the grim endeavour that must have gone into effecting its final downfall.

On Holy Island, off the Northumberland coast just south of the Scottish border, **Lindisfarne Castle** provides an example of a fortified structure that was allowed to fall into ruin and then, many years afterwards, restored because it was so picturesque and situated in such an attractive position.

The island was originally given over to monks, who despite continual raids by hostile Scots throughout the fourteenth and fifteenth centuries managed to maintain four churches with money they received from visitors. Under the dissolution of the monasteries of 1537 the priory was closed forcibly, and Henry VIII awarded it to himself. He did not oversee its upkeep, however, and before long it fell into ruin, the final ignominy coming in 1613 when Lord Walden had the roofs and lead bells removed. The ship carrying them away sank, which naturally led popular superstition to term the mishap an act of God.

Before this time, in 1543, Lord Hertford had led an expeditionary force against Scotland to mark disapproval of its alliance with France,

Corfe Castle

31

and he garrisoned 2,200 soldiers on Holy Island. Over the next few years some of the old priory ruins were fortified. Lindisfarne was never however an important fortress; when England and Scotland became united under James I it lost all importance even though it remained a fortress. During the Civil War the Parliamentarians gained control of it, though no battle was apparently fought over the prize and after the war it was allowed to return to its former somnolence. During the Jacobite rising of 1715 two Northumberland supporters of 'James III', Launcelot Errington and his nephew Mark, captured and held the valueless fortress for a brief spell and actually succeeded in raising 'James III's' flag.

During the early nineteenth century the castle became a coastguard station, later the headquarters of a detachment of Northumberland Artillery Volunteers. Its repeal came in 1900 when Edward Hudson, proprietor of *Country Life*, visited the island, saw its possibilities and decided to buy it. He then employed Sir Edwin Lutyens to supervise the castle's reconstruction.

Lutyens found various Tudor doorways and windows among the island's ruins; these he incorporated into the structure and finally fashioned from the old building two separate blocks set at right angles to one another. The rooms were filled with an assortment of antique furniture, so that today Lindisfarne—handed over to the care of the National Trust in 1944— presents the spectacle of an architectural curio in a most unusual setting, a far cry from its original purpose.

Scotland also boasts many fine castles, most of them erected in the form of castellated manor houses. One of the largest such building is **Glamis Castle** in Angus, famous for its

Lindisfarne Castle

Glamis Castle

legendary associations with Macbeth and for its Royal associations.

Tradition ascribes the foundation of Glamis to the tenth or eleventh century, but the oldest part of the present castle dates only from the fourteenth century, the creation of Sir John Lyon who in 1372 married a daughter of King Robert II and was made Thane of Glamis. Perhaps the most tragic event associated with the castle took place in 1537 when a Lady Glamis, falsely accused by a discarded suitor of witchcraft against James V, was dragged to her death at the stake on the Castle Hill in Edinburgh. In all probability Lady Glamis'

only real offence was to have been born a member of the clan Douglas, but as a result of her supposed treason the castle became forfeit to the Crown. Happily it was later restored to her son, whose descendant Patrick Lyon became Earl of Strathmore in 1677.

The castle is still the property of the Earls of Strathmore. It was here that Lady Elizabeth Bowes-Lyon, later to marry King George VI, was born; and here also, in 1930, that her second daughter Princess Margaret Rose was born, the first Royal child to be born in Scotland for some three centuries.

Another castellated mansion of typical Scottish design is **Craigievar Castle,** superbly situated overlooking the Leochel Burn and with a good claim to be one of the very finest examples of Scottish architecture. It stands seven storeys high, built in the form of a multi-turreted tower roughly the shape of the letter 'L', and was built in the year 1626 for a member of the Forbes family who enjoyed the nickname 'Willie the Merchant' and whose descendants still live at Craigievar.

The castle has benefitted from not being added to at all over the years. Inside it presents a superb spectacle, with the family motto of 'Doe not vaiken sleiping dogs' carved prominently on the arch of the main staircase. On the first floor the Great Hall has a fine ceiling bearing decorations in plaster relief of heraldry, foliage and classical portrait medallions; it possesses also a huge fireplace over which is placed a large Royal coat of arms, a fine example of one of the old timber screens once in common use and a musicians' gallery. There is also at Craigievar a Queen's Bedroom with a canopied bed and a delightful Blue Room.

Records of the Barony of Craigievar have been preserved in full, and it was the second Forbes laird who waged independent war on the freebooters who once plagued the surrounding countryside. Through his endeavours seven of these met their death by hanging at Edinburgh in 1636. A little after this the most notorious of them all, one Gilderoy, was captured. Over the years many of Gilderoy's deeds in Aberdeenshire have been attributed to Rob Roy Macgregor, but it is only a similarity in name that has caused confusion over this, and there is no foundation for the legend. Craigievar is above all else a beautiful building, picturesque in a way that is quite different from the grandeur of the traditional fortress.

Craigievar Castle

Harlech Castle

Harlech Castle in Merionethshire is a perfect example of the gauntest kind of military establishment, its blank walls unrelieved by superfluous ornament of any kind, its ruins leaving no doubt in the mind of the observer that Dafydd ap Ifan ap Einion and his men provided the inspiration for the traditional Welsh song 'Men of Harlech', having undergone severe hardship before surrendering to the Yorkists in the Wars of the Roses, the last stronghold to do so.

The building dates probably from 1285, being completed in 1290; but there is mention of a castle here long before the thirteenth century. Before its destruction Harlech was a massive square structure measuring approximately seventy yards along each side, with a round tower placed at each angle and one at either side of the main gateway. At the time of its construction the sea actually came right up to the rocks that form the base of the castle, which in addition to a moat hewn out of the rock should have given it pronounced security. Even so its history was one of continual siege.

Madoc ap Llewelyn attacked it in 1294-95, but on this occasion it held out with only a garrison of thirty seven men. Owen Glendower was more successful in 1404; he captured it and held his parliament there, a further stage in the rebellion he had launched during 1400 that was to give him eventual control of virtually the whole of North Wales. Following its Yorkist possession during the Wars of the Roses it was allowed to fall into decay, but active life returned to Harlech during the Civil War when after a prolonged siege it finally surrendered to Major General Mytton in 1647, the last castle in North Wales to do so.

35

Caernarvon Castle

Caernarvon Castle, somewhat to the north of Harlech, has enjoyed a similar history. Like Harlech, it was founded by Edward I, in the year 1283. It was completed by Edward's son, and its walls, which formerly enclosed the whole town, are still intact, anything between seven and nine feet in thickness and covering an area of some three acres.

Unlike Harlech, Caernarvon was never captured by Owen Glendower, though he twice besieged it. It was also more fortunate during the Civil War, for although it finally surrendered to the Parliamentarians in 1646 it did not suffer so much in a physical way. A warrant issued for its destruction in 1660 was fortunately never executed.

The name Caernarvon means 'The Fortress in Arvon'. It is extremely well preserved, benefitting from a restoration carried out a little over a century ago. Its original architect was one Henry de Elreton and this castle is generally regarded as his masterpiece. About its curtain walls are lofty towers bearing such names as the Eagle Tower, so named because an eagle was one of Edward I's crests, and the Queen's Tower, which once housed a banqueting hall but today contains the regimental museum of the Royal Welch Fusiliers. There is also a Well Tower, a Black Tower and finally Queen Eleanor's Gate, through which it is claimed King Edward's first wife entered the castle. Altogether there are nine towers and two double gatehouses.

Caernarvon Castle once provided a grim place of captivity for the notorious roundhead William Prynne, who was imprisoned here for an attack on Archbishop Laud of the Star Chamber. His penalty was severe in the extreme: he was fined £5,000 and sentenced to lose the remainder of his ears, to be branded on his cheeks and to be imprisoned here for life. Such barbarity is happily no longer practised, but it is not at all difficult, in contemplating this very large and heavily fortified castle, to call to mind such past customs.

Chapter Three
ECCLESIASTICAL

Over the centuries ecclesiastical foundations have contributed substantially to the storehouse of English architectural wonders. The great cathedrals of Britain are among its major treasures, a source of constant pleasure and delight. **Lincoln Cathedral** may certainly be counted among the most remarkable.

The present structure, described by John Ruskin in the nineteenth century as the finest in this country, was begun in 1072 by Bishop Remigius, the first Norman to be appointed to an English see after the Conquest. There was however an earlier building on the same site, built in 953 by the Saxons. In 1185 an unexpected earthquake shook Lincoln, and Remigius' building toppled to the ground. Only the west front and the Norman towers survived to be incorporated in the rebuilding, carried out under the supervision of St. Hugh of Lincoln.

As with all cathedrals, the building proceeded slowly, and it is likely that the marvellous choir that today bears St. Hugh's name was not completed until after his death. One of St. Hugh's successors to the bishopric was the Robert Grosseteste who wrote a treatise on optics, and it has been suggested that he may have provided the inspiration for the unusual double arcading to be seen along the lower part of the walls in the choir aisles and elsewhere, where an optical illusion gives the impression of two separate arcades with space between them, whereas in fact there is only a small recess in the walls.

Lincoln Cathedral possesses numerous wonders, but its west front is its particular glory, followed by the huge circular window paned by fragments of medieval glass above the south transept. There is also an attractive Chapter House and an exquisite High Altar setting that incorporates a stone canopy placed in position as late as the eighteenth century. And indeed a tendency to add new features has always been a tradition at Lincoln, most recently in the small chapel dedicated to St. Blaise, patron saint of the wool industry, where

there are murals by Duncan Grant, completed in 1958.

The cathedral library is another of its major possessions, housing numerous rare old books and more than 240 medieval manuscripts, as

Lincoln Cathedral, West Front

York Minster

well as the Lincoln copy of the Magna Carta. It is however for its physical properties that Lincoln is best remembered, for it is one of the wonders of Gothic architecture, set in a position of such eminence and splendour that it is impossible not to be always aware of its presence in the city that was settled even in Roman times, and where Roman remains are still being uncovered.

Equal to Lincoln is **York Minster,** also dominating a city that was important in Roman times. The present building, dedicated to St. Peter, was initiated in 1080 following the appointment of Thomas of Bayeux as Archbishop of York; however, the ecclesiastical associations of its present location stem back to the early seventh century, when St. Augustine appointed Paulinus to be Bishop of York. Building and rebuilding continued at intervals up until 1227, and then it was decided that the cathedral should be completely reconstructed. Thus it is that today, with the exception of the old crypt, no part of the building can be dated before that year.

For the student of architecture this is of primary significance, for it follows that in York Minster it is possible to inspect a first class example of pure late medieval architecture as it developed (the massive central tower was not completed until early in the fifteenth century). Its west front is this building's major feature, even though the huddle of buildings standing before it has made it difficult to secure an unobstructed view. The twin towers were added at a slightly later date than the original fourteenth century front, but they blend perfectly with the rest of the structure and with the decorative exuberance of the whole.

York is an immense building, and it is the interior that causes one to acknowledge this most forcibly. The nave, for instance, is the highest and broadest of any cathedral in England. Begun in 1291, it took until 1338 for it to be completed. The Chapter House also is

38

on a grand scale, erected between 1290 and 1310; it is unusual not only for its great size but in addition for the absence of any central vaulting pier and for the large amount of glass. These fineries apart, York's famous stained glass windows attract perhaps the largest measure of attention, for within this wonderful building is to be found the largest concentration of medieval glass to be seen anywhere in the country, almost all of it of the very highest quality, and of especial interest because it allows an assessment of the progress of glass painting throughout the whole of the middle ages. The glow of light and colour that was then considered to be an integral part of ecclesiastical atmosphere may still be wondered at.

Quite a way north of York is **Durham Cathedral,** another major achievement in Church architecture. Some people hold this to be the most perfectly proportioned of all English cathedrals, but this is only one of its claims to distinction: its Anglo-Norman features are superb, and it has the added interest of being built on the site of a little church once built by the followers of St. Cuthbert, a crude wooden structure, the last of several put up by them as they moved about the country. Two years later a stone church was completed; then in 1093 the Norman bishop, William of St. Carileph, laid the foundations of a Benedictine abbey church, the whole of which required until 1133 to be completed.

This is the building one sees today, though there have been additions over the years. The twin towers that look out from their eminence over the river are only part Norman, for instance, and were heightened during the thirteenth century; while the fine and somewhat gaunt central tower was not added until 1474.

At the extreme eastern end of the building is an addition of 1242 known as the Chapel of the Nine Altars. It was here, in the cathedral's early days, that the shrine to St. Cuthbert, removed from the old wooden church, was placed. The shrine has disappeared since then, but what can be seen in this chapel is a carved head on the wall arcade of the man responsible for its masonry, one Richard of Farnham.

Between St. Cuthbert's shrine and the High Altar was placed a great stone screen, built during the 1370's and still in existence. This was the gift of Lord Neville of Raby Castle, constructed from Dorset stone and transported from London to Newcastle by sea.

Durham has alas suffered a certain amount of disfigurement over the centuries. In 1650 the Scottish prisoners taken at Dunbar were confined here, and duly set about destroying the choir stalls; these were replaced soon afterwards and are still as they then were. During the nineteenth century the cathedral suffered even further disaster, this time in the form of 'restoration'. Fortunately all the principal grandeur remains; and most important of all to some, so does the ancient association with the Venerable Bede, the early Church historian, whose remains lie buried in the Lady Chapel.

Durham Cathedral

Chester Cathedral is another notable Norman foundation, but one that to some slight extent, at least from the outside, belies its antiquity. It was built originally from red sandstone, one of the materials most affected by the elements over the years, which factor has entailed a good deal of patching and encasing from time to time. However, the cathedral dates back to 1093, when building was begun

Chester Cathedral

under the auspices of Hugh Lupus, Earl of Chester and Lord of the Welsh Marches. He planned it as a Benedictine monastery, but Henry VIII created it a cathedral church, one of six new sees he established after the dissolution of the monasteries.

Of the original building only parts have survived. Much rebuilding took place between the years 1200 and 1315, including the remodelling of the entire eastern limb and the Lady Chapel; later, in the fourteenth century, there were further enlargements, but unfortunately work was interrupted by the Black Death and only resumed during the following century. Those parts of the original Norman building still standing are the north transept, parts of the north west tower and the north wall of the nave aisle; all other parts date from either of the major rebuilding periods mentioned above.

The interior of Chester Cathedral, and especially the nave, is majestic. In the Lady Chapel today is preserved an ancient shrine to St. Werburgh; it is no longer complete, but it is of interest to learn that when it was, and was housed in the north transept, it provided both cathedral and city with its major tourist attraction and, it is said, for a long time provided the cathedral with its main source of income. Today the beauty of the building itself is the principal attraction.

The smallest episcopal city in England is Ely in Cambridgeshire. **Ely Cathedral,** dedicated to the Holy and Undivided Trinity, dates in its present guise from 1080, the building taking over a century and a half to accomplish. However, the ecclesiastical history of the small city extends back as far as the year 673, when Etheldreda, Princess of East Anglia, founded a religious establishment that was then in her own possession but is now covered by this superb cathedral.

Following its completion, like so many other fine buildings, the cathedral awaited tragedy; it came in 1322, when the great central tower collapsed and destroyed as it did so a large part of the eastern limb. Fortunately there was on the spot at the time one Alan of Walsingham, sub-prior and later sacrist, who in his capacity as custodian of the fabric was given the responsiblity of seeing to the cathedral's repair.

Ely Cathedral

The choir and Lady Chapel, both of them rich in decorative carving that is acknowledged to be among the finest in England, were both initiated by Walsingham; so was one of the cathedral's most characteristic external features, the large Octagon above the crossing, a worthy neighbour to the great western tower. The construction of this Octagon must be regarded as a considerable architectural feat, twelve years being required for its completion. While it was being built the roads into Ely had to be specially strengthened to bear the burden of the massive pieces of oak that invisibly support the timber vaulting, each beam being 63 feet in length and three feet square.

Ely's other marvel is its wonderful nave, completed towards the close of the twelfth century. The western tower is also a superb piece of work, completed in the fourteenth century and incorporating tier upon tier of intricate arcading that varies according to the era of building, the overall effect demonstrating a development away from the romanesque style in favour of the full-lancet. This tower, like the Octagon and indeed the whole of this unusually long building, set amid flat countryside and visible for miles around, is equally impressive when viewed from a distance.

Ely's counterpart in Wales is **St. David's Cathedral,** set in what is technically a city but in effect no more than a very small town. This fine cathedral, a mile away from the sea, originated as a monastic church, and its oldest part, the nave, dates from the latter part of the twelfth century when the entire cathedral had to be rebuilt following its destruction by the Danes in 1078.

This was not the only tragedy to befall the building; in 1220 the tower collapsed, destroying the choir and transepts and necessitating further rebuilding. A Lady Chapel was added in about 1300, a fine rood screen—now carefully restored—during the fourteenth century and some still existing choir stalls during the fifteenth century. A shrine to St. David is preserved in the west bay of the north side of the presbytery and another shrine, to St. Caradoc (who died in 1124), in the wall of the north transept.

St. David's is built out of stone that is of a purplish slate colour, having been transported from Caerbwdy; some slightly redder stone came from Caerfai. Within there is a fine transitional Norman nave, and on the fourth and fifth piers on the south side are the remains of some ancient wall paintings. There is a fine cathedral library; while close by are the ruins of an old Bishop's Palace, erected by Bishop Gower in 1340 and one of the first such buildings in Great Britain.

Unique to St. David's, and certainly worthy of notice, is the fact that the reigning sovereign of Great Britain holds the first cursal prebendal stall in the choir, and this is adorned by a carved and painted Royal coat of arms. For some reason the stall was never once occupied by a monarch until 1955, when Queen Elizabeth II visited the cathedral.

St. David's is perhaps most universally known for being situated in the smallest city in Great Britain. **Salisbury Cathedral** in Wiltshire is similarly most widely known for a purely incidental reason. This is of course for the fact that John Constable painted it so skilfully and at the same time evocatively, from a distance on the opposite bank of the Avon, which is still the most impressive prospect of all. The high spire (the highest in England) dominates the countryside; it was not however a part of the original plan for the building, which was begun under Bishop Poore in 1220 and consecrated in the presence of Henry III in 1258. Both it and the upper part of the tower were added early in the fourteenth century.

St. David's Cathedral

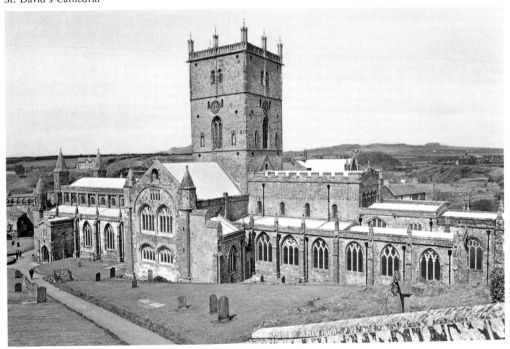

Having caused the spire to be erected, those responsible for the upkeep of the building were perpetually worried lest it should collapse. During the fifteenth century, as a result, both flying buttresses and internal stone girders at the crossing were added; but it was only in 1697 that a final strengthening of the entire building was undertaken under the supervision of Sir Christopher Wren. Thereafter the only destruction Salisbury could suffer would come from human hands. This duly happened in 1798, when James Wyatt superintended the demolition of a good deal of internal structure in order to provide what he termed 'vistas', a procedure that also called for the removal of much of the fine stained glass. Then in 1862 Gilbert Scott completed the havoc by adding the trappings of Victorian ecclesiastical decoration that are associated with his name.

Happily the cathedral's glory, its exterior, remains unchanged. The spire is 404 feet in height; it stands atop a central tower that shows off fourteenth century craftsmanship to perfection; and even if the west front has been criticised for the superfluous character of some of its decoration, it nevertheless graces the building impressively. The statues filling the numerous niches in the front are not the originals, which were disfigured by time and the elements, but they at least give an indication of how the front might have looked in earlier days.

A similar operation has recently been mounted on **Wells Cathedral** in Somerset, nestling beneath the Mendip Hills and traditionally established in the year 705, though no records exist prior to 909 in which year it was accorded cathedral rank. Soon after this it was completely rebuilt, and then reconstructed again under the direction of Bishop Robert Lewes during the fourth and fifth decades of the twelfth century. Even this building was

Salisbury Cathedral

thought in need of reworking later in the twelfth century, under Bishop Reginald de Bohun; it is the building as he conceived it that one may inspect today.

Like Lincoln, the particular glory of Wells is its west front, with its array of medieval figure carving that has led more than one admirer to declare that the entire facade is really one large-scale piece of stone sculpture, almost perfectly proportioned. The figures, not all of which are scheduled for restoration, range from saints and priests to bishops and kings, to noblemen and legendary characters and finally to the central figure of Christ himself.

Wells enjoys delightful surroundings, including a cluster of miscellaneous ecclesiastical buildings that have a charm all of their own, especially the Tudor Bishop's Palace. Perhaps it falls short of such establishments as Lincoln and York in grandeur, but in its own way it is perfect.

After so many fine cathedral buildings it is appropriate to glance at something a little more humble, yet no less attractive because of that. The building in question is the **Parish Church of Stoke Poges** in Buckinghamshire, famous for Thomas Gray's having conceived his famous 'Elegy Written in a Country Churchyard' within the confines of this very churchyard, his name being now permanently associated with the village of Stoke Poges.

His poem is perhaps the best remembered in the English language, and his tomb, alongside that of his mother, is to be inspected in the churchyard. The link with Gray should not however blind visitors to the church's other interesting and pleasing features—the fact, for instance, that it blends Saxon, Norman, early Gothic and Tudor architectural styles.

The church is dedicated to St. Giles; its Saxon remains are to be seen in part of the chancel wall and its window. The Norman

Wells Cathedral, West Front

Stoke Poges Parish Church, Hastings Chapel

additions and alterations date from the year 1086, but about 1220 the nave was reconstructed on the original Norman pillars. Even more emphatic in terms of refurbishing was the removal, possibly on account of its narrowness, of the Norman chancel arch in 1844.

In 1338 Sir John de Molyns founded a chantry in the church, and his tomb can be seen today within the left side of the chancel wall. But surely the most impressive of all the architectural features in this pleasing little church, with fine old oak roof supports prominent in both porch and nave, is the Hastings Chapel, built in 1558 by Lord Hastings of Loughborough, son of the first Earl of Huntingdon.

This chapel in red brick was erected to serve the inmates of a local almshouse; it was successfully restored in 1946-48 and today constitutes one of the finest such Tudor chapels to be found anywhere in the country. Its memorials include a mural monument of the early eighteenth century bearing no inscription as to whom it commemorates, though it is thought possibly to have been erected in memory of Sir Thomas and Sir Walter Clarges.

One further interesting feature of Stoke Poges Church is its short cloister, part of a private entrance to the church from the nearby manor and joining the vestibule with the main building. There are numerous other attractive aspects of this little church and it is a most fitting building to be illustrated in these pages.

Of the numerous ruined abbeys that make up another aspect of ecclesiastical architecture surely the most spectacular is **Fountains Abbey** in Yorkshire. Even in the completeness of its survival it surpasses all others. A Cistercian foundation, it was given early in the twelfth century by Archbishop Thurstan to twelve Benedictine monks who had opted to observe Cistercian austerity; it lies in an isolated spot in a narrow wooded valley of the river Skell, ideal for the cloistered and self-sufficient rule of life favoured by this order.

Fountains Abbey

Tradition says that the old yews above the thirteenth century mill gave the twelve men their first shelter, but they were not long in supervising their abbey's erection, for the gatehouse dates from the twelfth century and the church from the years 1134-1247, though its great tower rising to a height of 168 feet was built much later, in Tudor times, by Abbot Huby. Much of this fine building, including its outer walls and the arches of the spectacular nave which extends for some 370 feet, still stands, and its glory is hardly at all diminished.

The view along the nave culminates, as one stands at the west door, in the great 60 foot east window built during the fifteenth century. This is itself complemented by a great west window built by Abbot Darnton about 1494. The cloisters have disappeared, but many of the buildings about them have survived, most conspicuously the two vast passages, each 300 feet in extent, that run side by side on the west side of the cloisters towards the Skell. This most impressive structure is made up from nineteen central pillars from which ribs of vaulting spread like huge branches down to the ground on both sides to form an immense hall lighted by small windows. This is known as the cellarium, and was built in three compartments, one of which may have been a refectory.

Among Cistercian foundations **Tintern Abbey,** on the banks of the Wye in Monmouthshire, stands almost equally supreme. The abbey was founded in 1131 by Walter FitzRichard, Lord of Lower Gwent and Striguil, but the greater part of what remains for inspection today dates from 1220 and later, in which year enlargement took place.

The principal building among these additions was the magnificent church, credited to the patronage of Roger Bigod, Earl of Norfolk and still sufficiently intact to be fully appreciated. The striking nave is its principal feature,

46

Tintern Abbey

with a great east window that is now no more than a shell.

Tintern suffered like all other monasteries when Henry VIII ordered their dissolution, but fortunately it lay in an isolated position and its stones were not easily removable, as elsewhere, for other purposes. Later the Dukes of Beaufort, whose property it had become, took an interest in the abbey's preservation (though latterly only as a 'picturesque ruin') and thus it was that by the eighteenth century, when tourists began to seek out such establishments, it was still in a tolerably recognisable condition. More recent excavations have revealed extensive remains.

Tintern has provided subject matter for numerous landscape painters over the centuries, and because of its setting this is not surprising. Closer examination of individual features however, reveals much of architectural interest, as well as numerous incidental apart-

ments that even though they are in a condition of dilapidation still vividly bring to life something of the now vanished monastic existence that was once led here. Surviving parts range from the old kitchen to an ancient guest house.

An interesting Benedictine foundation is **Pershore Abbey,** founded as long ago as 689. In that year Ethelred, King of Mercia, gave the site to his nephew Oswald in order to establish a religious house. This building was destroyed by the Danes in 958; it was rebuilt as a Benedictine monastery in 972, being granted a charter by King Edgar.

The abbey enjoyed considerable prosperity, but following the Norman Conquest it fell on hard times, many of its treasures being confiscated first of all by the Conqueror and later by Edward the Confessor, the latter of whom devoted the money raised towards the building of Westminster Abbey.

47

Pershore Abbey

Fires, in 1223 and 1288, destroyed much of the original fabric at Pershore, and the present structure dates in the main from the years immediately following the second fire. From that time forward until the year 1534, when Pershore was dissolved by Henry VIII, the abbey enjoyed a relatively uninterrupted life. Henry VIII allowed the nave of the church and all the domestic buildings to be destroyed, and all that now remain are the choir and transepts, saved by the townsfolk at the time of the dissolution when they collected some £400 towards the cost of repairs.

What remains is wholly impressive. The fine roof vaulting dates from just after 1288; but of earlier date than this is the south transept, which miraculously escaped both fires and is the oldest part of the abbey. It was probably erected at the instigation of Duke Odda, who died in 1056. In this part of the abbey are to be found the tombs of a Knight Templar of about the year 1250 and of Abbot William de Herrington, who died in 1340.

Another survivor from earlier times is a fine ornamented Norman font, returned to the abbey in 1921 after having been used first of all as a cattle trough and then as a garden ornament. Most of the other notable features at Pershore are of later date, including several interesting monuments. A nineteenth century addition, the work of Gilbert Scott, is the well known 'Cat's Cradle' bell-ringers' platform at the top of the lovely fourteenth century lantern tower.

This tower, indeed, is one of the abbey's principal glories, standing on four Norman arches, the only survivors in this part of the building of the fire of 1288 which destroyed the older tower. The new tower was completed about 1335, and many people hold it to be one of the most beautiful in Great Britain. Outside it rises to a height of 114 feet.

The exterior of Pershore is also of considerable appeal; but perhaps the most intriguing features are the numerous hints of now vanished parts of the abbey, ranging from the tree-lined pathway leading to the west door that marks the site of the original nave, to the two small cottages just outside the main churchyard that were at one time the almonry of the monastery.

It is an easy matter to select another Benedictine foundation for inclusion here, for **Glastonbury Abbey** in Somerset has the distinction of being the oldest Christian sanctuary in England and is associated with numerous colourful legends. Principal among these is of course that Joseph of Arimathea brought the Holy Grail with him to this establishment; this was supposedly a receptacle containing some of the blood as well as sweat of Jesus Christ, and became the subject matter for a remarkable amount of literary invention over the centuries.

It is difficult to arrive at a date of origin, but there was a church on the site of the present abbey long before the Saxons came to Britain, built by Christian missionaries in a part of the country then known as Avalon. Probably this occurred during the second or third century, but over the years the date was gradually moved back in popular imagination to the first century A.D. By the beginning of the eighth century the church had passed into the hands of the Christianised Saxons, the only religious establishment to do so.

During the fifth century both St. Patrick and St. Benignus are supposed to have resided here. St. Bridget is also associated with Glastonbury; and so is St. David, who in 546 built an addition to the old church. St. Dunstan became abbot in 945, and established a strict form of life; in fact he is credited with having consolidated the Benedictine rule in Britain, which before this time had not been observed at all seriously. Other abbots followed, and the abbey both prospered and grew. Then, in 1184, fire descended and destroyed the entire complex, including the original church.

What can be seen today are the ruined remains of the rebuilt foundation, whose chapel was consecrated in 1186-87. The great abbey church, dedicated to St. Peter and St. Paul was begun about this time also, and work on it continued throughout the thirteenth and fourteenth centuries.

The last abbot of Glastonbury was Richard Whiting: he refused to surrender his abbey to Henry VIII at the time of the suppression of the monasteries, and because of it was executed, on an unjustifiable charge of embezzlement, on Glastonbury Tor on November 15, 1539.

As a last example of the monastic edifices of Britain it is fitting to turn to Scotland, to the Cistercian **Melrose Abbey** in Berwickshire on the southern bank of the Tweed. Like many others in Scotland, this abbey was founded by David I; it was occupied first of all by monks from Rievaulx in Yorkshire.

It suffered destruction at the hands of Edward II, but was rebuilt under the patronage of the Bruce, despite periodic attacks by Richard II. Much of the present structure

Glastonbury Abbey

Melrose Abbey

dates from the fifteenth and sixteenth centuries but in 1544 it was reduced by the Earl of Hertford and thereafter fell into a state of decay, its stones being plundered for various purposes over the ensuing decades; by the Douglas family, for instance, into whose hands it fell in 1568 and who used much of the masonry to build a private house at the end of the cloisters. Melrose was finally restored in 1822, under the supervision of Sir Walter Scott and the patronage of the Duke of Buccleuch, who gave it to the nation.

What does survive is of great beauty; the variety of carved capitals is a particularly notable feature. There are also impressive windows in the transepts, and a great east window. Beneath the High Altar at the foot of the east window the heart of the Bruce is said to have been buried; Alexander II's remains are also buried in the abbey, and there are several tombs of the Douglas family. There is much else at Melrose, but as with all other abbeys described here, it is for its hint of past grandeur that it most claims attention today.

50

Chapter Four
MISCELLANEOUS

The historic buildings already described in these pages all fall into particular categories, but they do not in any way constitute the entire spectrum of interesting historic buildings to be found in Great Britain. There are, for instance, town halls and other civic buildings, colleges, even inns, and many are deserving of mention. There is space here only for a brief selection to complement what has already been described, and an apt building with which to start is the **Guildhall at Lavenham** in Suffolk.

This is a fine old half-timbered building that has experienced something of a chequered history, having survived the centuries not in its original capacity but as a curio and historical relic. In point of fact it ceased to be a guildhall soon after the suppression of the monasteries,

and although it had only been erected in 1529, by 1600 it had become parish property.

The guild it was built to serve was that of Corpus Christi a trade guild established in Suffolk some two centuries previously to further the wool trade. However, as the name would suggest, members of the guild were also firmly rooted in religious observation and Church festivities, and it was this fact that caused it to perish under Henry VIII's urgent fury.

Throughout the seventeenth century the old guildhall was employed as a town hall; later it was used as a prison, a workhouse and finally, and aptly enough, a wool store. Throughout this period it was allowed to fall into a condition of disrepair, and a good deal of the interior decoration disappeared for ever. Fortunately in

Guildhall, Lavenham

1887 Sir Cuthbert Quilter took an interest in what is certainly one of the best examples of a sixteenth century half-timbered public building in the country, and undertook its restoration. In 1951 the building came into the hands of the National Trust, and now it is assured of preservation, a notable monument to the extravagance and presumably considerable affluence of those sixteenth century Suffolk merchants.

A much less ostentatious building of the same kind is **Thaxted Guildhall** in Essex, standing at the heart of a town that to this day wears much of its medieval aspect and boasts many fine half-timbered cottages and an interesting parish church of St. John.

This guildhall is older than that at Lavenham, but only marginally so, dating from the year 1475. It is a three-storeyed structure, constructed in such a way that each storey overhangs the one beneath it, topped by a divided sloping roof. The ground floor is open, supported by stout wooden struts.

In recent years the guildhall has been completely renovated, rendering it one of the best preserved buildings of this nature in Britain, an attractive reminder of a past age and a structure of considerable charm in its own right.

Among the smaller civic buildings scattered throughout Britain that date from the seventeenth and eighteenth centuries few are as attractive to look at as Christopher Kempster's **Town Hall at Abingdon** in Berkshire, a centre of the wool trade and at one time the county

Guildhall, Thaxted

Town Hall, Abingdon

town until Reading assumed the privilege.

The town hall was erected over the period 1677-82, under the supervision of Kempster but designed by an unknown architect, and it has frequently been asserted that the architect was in fact Sir Christopher Wren. Certainly the building is worthy of his style. It consists of two storeys, together with cellars and an attic; today the market hall is situated on the ground floor, inside the open arcade, while the large first floor is used as a courtroom.

The entire structure bears the hallmark of a master architect, built to graceful proportions. Tall Corinthian pilasters, sixteen in number, extend the height of the building; the whole is topped by a sloping roof with generous coping, a decorative cupola and balustrade. The interior is surprisingly spacious, and the courtroom measures 57 feet by 37 feet.

Abingdon is an historic old town, containing several interesting buildings, ranging from old almshouses to the late seventeenth century county hall, built in the year following the town hall's completion, yet the town hall, adjoining the market place, has contrived to attract most attention, specifically because of its architectural attractiveness.

On a totally different scale from these three buildings, but also classifiable under the general category of civic buildings, is **St. George's Hall, Liverpool,** standing at the heart of a city that, outside London, is one of Britain's foremost cultural and trading centres. Liverpool is an important port and industrial city, and because of this it suffered severe bomb damage during the Second World War. It is therefore more than fortunate that this building, together with other fine public buildings, should have survived.

St. George's Hall dates back to the year 1842, and is the work of Harvey Lonsdale Elmes, who died in 1847 at the early age of 34,

St. George's Hall, Liverpool

long before work on his masterpiece had been completed. Thus, although the design for the great vault was Elmes' own, it was in fact completed by Sir Robert Rawlinson. Both the exterior and the interior decoration were carried out by C. R. Cockerell. The building was finally inaugurated in 1854, on the anniversary of Queen Victoria's coronation.

One of the most notable civic buildings in England, built in imitation of a classical temple on a massive scale, St. George's Hall was originally conceived as two separate buildings, to be built partly by public subscription. Finally Elmes had the idea of combining law courts and a concert hall within one shell, and the money collected by public subscription was refunded to the donors, the city of Liverpool meeting the full expense of the building.

Today St. George's Hall is employed mainly for judicial purposes, but it is still used as a concert hall, the main hall seating some 1,800 people and the concert room 725. It possesses extremely fine tessellated floors and a great organ of unusually large dimensions.

The interior of the hall is sumptuous, a worthy monument to the affluent Liverpool of the nineteenth century; its outward appearance also demands admiration, commandingly positioned in the city centre. Several pieces of statuary surround the hall, including representations of both Queen Victoria and her Consort.

Further south, in **King's Lynn** in Norfolk, there survives in even greater forcefulness the flavour of a past era of prosperity; for this one time highly important port on the Great Ouse boasts some of the finest commercial architecture, most of it dating from the late seventeenth and early eighteenth centuries, to be found in any comparable town in England, with lovely buildings that range from hotels to the fine guildhall and the **Old Custom House.**

This lovely little structure on Purfleet Quay, facing out over the harbour it was built to serve, like so much else in this unusual town, is reminiscent of the Dutch in appearance. Erected in 1683, it is the work of a local architect by the name of Henry Bell, who was also responsible for the impressive Duke's Head Hotel.

Its characteristic appearance derives from the classical lines of its two lower storeys, being surmounted by a roof with projecting windows and a dignified lantern tower. That so grandiose a building was conceived and erected as a mere custom house marks more surely than anything else the high volume of trade that this busy port handled in those days, particularly with the Low Countries.

Both Norfolk and Suffolk lie in that part of the country which is known as East Anglia. Huntingdonshire also falls into this pocket of territory, and in the village of **Houghton,** at the side of the Great Ouse, there stands another interesting old building that acts as a monument to a past era. This is the old **Mill,** one of the best preserved examples of this type of architecture to be found anywhere in Britain, thought to be the oldest mill on the Ouse. Its wonderful situation beside the river lends it an additional attraction in the form of picturesqueness, lying on the fringe of a lovely village rich in thatched cottages.

Today Houghton Mill is the property of the National Trust, having been given to it in 1939 by the River Ouse Catchment Board and the borough councils of Huntingdon and Godmanchester. It is now leased to the Youth Hostels Association, and because of this there has been added to it an outside fire escape, the only portion of the structure that is not as originally built.

The mill wheel has disappeared over the years, but it is still easy to picture this building when it was in active use to grind corn. There has in recent years been an upsurge of interest in relics of the industrial past, and well do such buildings as Houghton Mill warrant the description 'historic'. It is gratifying that this very firm reminder of a past age has been so well preserved.

The **Lord Leycester Hospital in Warwick** stands as a reminder of yet another character-istic of the past, a foundation on a very much smaller scale and a good deal older than the famous Royal Hospital in London, home of the Chelsea Pensioners. It was founded by Robert Dudley, first Earl of Leycester and intimate friend of Queen Elizabeth I.

Long before this, in 1123, the then Earl of Warwick presented the small Chapel of St. James, the oldest building in the group now making up the hospital, to the Church of St. Mary. The chapel later became a centre for the

Old Custom House, King's Lynn

Houghton Mill

Guild of St. George the Martyr; while the Guild, whose hall is still in existence here, became amalgamated with other guilds to form the United Guilds of Warwick in 1383 and was granted a royal charter. In 1571 Robert Dudley acquired the buildings, founding a hospital under a charter granted by his Queen soon after.

The hospital was instituted for the purpose of accommodating Dudley's aged or infirm retainers and their wives, the corporation consisting of a Master and twelve Brethren, and was endowed with £200 annually. Parts of the buildings were then converted into apartments of two rooms each, which arrangement persisted until 1950, when the Guildhall was cleared and the number of residents was temporarily reduced to five.

In 1956 an Act of Parliament replaced the earlier arrangement with a Board of Governors, who set about restoring the building to its present very fine condition, at the same time modernising the housing arrangements of the Brethren, a task which was completed in 1966.

The buildings themselves are wonderfully redolent of medieval times. The Guildhall—with its display of swords and trophies brought home by various Brethren from the campaigns of their employer—and the Great Hall of King James—dating from 1383 and taking its name from the occasion in 1617 when James I held a banquet here—both display fine old beams; while the courtyard, with its cloisters, is a truly lovely retreat. Here is to be found the Master's House, built at some date prior to 1400.

The coats of arms displayed on the outside of the buildings surrounding the courtyard are of interest. They include the arms and devices of Lord Leycester himself (a bear and a ragged staff) and of the Sidney family (a porcupine), together with the shields of various families with which the Sidneys have had connections.

56

Lord Leycester Hospital, Courtyard

57

Like Warwick, **Bath** has always been one of the more important English provincial centres; it is also of course a famous spa, and during the eighteenth century in the days of Beau Nash it glittered socially in a way that even Brighton was hard pressed to rival. Nash it was indeed who moulded Bath society, dictated what people of fashion and rank could do or not do, what they should wear, what dances they should dance. It is more than fitting therefore that a statue of this famous dandy should grace the **Great Pump Room,** adjoining the famous Roman baths.

The hot mineral springs to which Bath owes its prosperity consist of lime carbonated water, discovered to be effective in the cure of numerous diseases and used for either drinking or bathing. The healing properties of these waters were discovered long before the Romans came to Britain, but they were the ones who established Bath, who built the famous baths there and laid the foundations for its future prosperity.

The Great Pump Room was erected during 1796, a large classical building that is today partly given over to a museum. Mineral waters were served in a separate alcove, graced by stained glass windows that bear scenes from the history of Bath and containing a statuette of the angel at the pool of Bethesda. At times the spring waters rose to quite high temperatures, and as this occurred water was taken from adjoining baths to cool them.

Great Pump Room, Bath

Ye Olde Trip to Jerusalem

The Pump Room, however, during the eighteenth and nineteenth centuries, was not merely a place where health-giving waters were dispensed; it was also one of the social centres of Bath, where people of fashion might congregate to pass away a few hours of the morning in idle conversation before proceeding to more formal social pleasures later in the day. In this respect it can be regarded as one of the more important structures—graceful in its own right —in what has always been one of the most genteel of English cities, the summer domicile of many notable men and women of a past era.

Ordinary Englishmen took their pleasure in less graceful establishments than the Great Pump Room at Bath, more often than not in inns and taverns. In view of this, no publication dealing with British historic buildings could fail to illustrate one of the country's old inns. Several such establishments spring to mind, but here **Ye Olde Trip to Jerusalem in Nottingham** has been selected, dating back at least to the year 1189.

The word 'trip' or 'tryppe', meant originally a 'halt' or resting place, and this old tavern derives its name from the fact that crusaders on their way to fight alongside Richard I in the Holy Land paused here for refreshment. The date 1189 can thus be applied with certainty.

The building itself is of fascinating construction, for in parts it is literally hewn out of the rock, nestling beneath Nottingham's famous old castle, its small rooms having originally been no more than what amounted to a series of interconnected caves. The rock from which the small chambers are fashioned is so porous that spilt beverages disappear from view even before there is time to mop them up; and it is this great softness of course that has facilitated the house's extension from time to time.

Among other unusual features the Trip to Jerusalem boasts a rock-hewn secret passage, known as 'Mortimer's Hole', so named because it is said that the young King Edward III and his followers gained entrance to the castle by means of it in order to seize Roger Mortimer, Earl of March and paramour of Queen Isabella. This occurred in the year 1330; later that year Mortimer was executed at Tyburn.

Although the Trip to Jerusalem can only be dated with confidence to 1189, even before that time it probably served as the brewhouse to the castle, abutting on what is still known as Brewhouse Yard, one of the most fascinating spots in Nottingham and at one time notorious for the unsavoury character of many of its frequenters.

Today this inn is a popular tourist attraction, a unique tavern in every sense of the word. It boasts very firm reminders of antiquity, ranging from the narrow aperture in the cellars that is said to have been a speaking tube between the inn and the castle, once employed by Knights Templars, to the very aroma of the building's interior, the musty smell of many

Thomas Hardy's Birthplace

centuries of existence, made more pronounced by its peculiar construction.

Totally dissimilar to the last building, and indeed quite different from the other properties illustrated in this book, is **Thomas Hardy's Birthplace, Higher Bockhampton,** Dorset, the lovely cottage in an idyllic setting where the future novelist grew up and acquired the love of nature that characterises his fiction.

Hardy was born in the year 1840 in a cottage built by his grandfather. It looks today much as it would have done then save for the fact that the original masonry of chalk, clay, straw and other materials favoured in west country building at the time has been given a brick facing to protect it from the weather. The novelist lived here until he was twenty two years of age, when he travelled to London and remained there five years; he returned however to the place of his birth, and he continued to visit the cottage at intervals right through his life, making his last visit in 1926.

By that time Hardy had acquired the stature of a major novelist that has undergone a process of consolidation ever since. By 1948 his birthplace was thought to be of sufficient historic value to be maintained by the National Trust, which duly acquired it. Since then it has been transformed into a small Hardy museum containing several items connected with the novelist, a worthy memento of the author of *Tess of the D'Urbervilles* and other masterpieces.

One other class of building that may be considered in an historic context can be loosely defined as educational. Oxford and Cambridge among the university cities come immediately to mind, both of them so rich in lovely old colleges that it is difficult to make a representative choice; but surely **King's College, Cambridge,** with its wonderful chapel, calls for inclusion here.

Founded by King Henry VI in 1440, the same year that he founded Eton College, with which it has close associations, King's College is one of Cambridge's especial glories; its chapel, its most lovely possession, dates from the years 1446-1515, containing what is surely one of the finest perpendicular interiors in Great Britain, with stained glass windows that

60

King's College Chapel, Cambridge

with one exception date from the sixteenth century and a fan-vaulted ceiling that lends to the whole interior a calm grandeur that with careful cleaning has acquired a truly magnificent aspect. Other attractions within this chapel include the carved stalls and organ screen.

If the chapel is this college's most famous sight it does not in any way constitute the sole building worthy of inspection. Both the Great Court and the Fellows' Building are fine collegiate structures, though all the other buildings connected with this college are of more recent date, erected during the eighteenth and nineteenth centuries. It is not however buildings so much as eminent students of the past that constitute a college's calibre, and among other members of King's one can cite Archbishop Sumner, Sir William Temple, Sir Robert Walpole and Horace Walpole.

Since both Eton and King's Colleges are of the same foundation, it is of interest to note that under new statutes made out for Eton in 1443 King's was to take its students exclusively from the famous school. This no longer applies of course, but even so there are still links between the two establishments, just as there are between other Oxford and Cambridge colleges and certain of the older-established schools.

Oxford and Cambridge are so naturally bracketed together that King's must necessarily be complemented here by the choice of an Oxford college, but one of a totally different nature: for **All Souls College** does not admit undergraduates, only graduates. This is not unique at Oxford, for St. Anthony's and Nuffield colleges are constituted in exactly the same way, though their expressed aims are somewhat different.

All Souls was founded in 1437 by Henry Chichele, Archbishop of Canterbury; his co-founder was Henry VI. The college is dedicated particularly to those who fell during the

61

All Souls College, Oxford

Hundred Years War. It possesses a number of notable features, including a gatehouse erected during 1438 and a front quadrangle that has been virtually unaltered ever since 1441. The chapel dates from 1442, a perpendicular Gothic structure with a most impressive interior. The four east windows of the ante chapel contain all original glass, while later additions to the building include such items as a massive screen of black and gold that dates from the seventeenth century. The choir stalls contain particularly fine misericords.

The original structure included a lovely library (no longer used as such) whose treasures, many of which were lost or destroyed at the time of the Reformation, still include a Coverdale Bible. A newer building, the Codrington Library, has replaced this, completed in the year 1756 and boasting a main reading room that is some 200 feet in length.

Other later additions include the Warden's Lodgings, built during 1704-06, the great quadrangle with its twin towers that are the college's most easily identifiable features, erected between 1714 and 1734, and the Hall, built in 1730. Like so many of the other Oxford colleges, All Souls is a feast for the architectural enthusiast.

Today its constitution is sedate and its Fellows all academics of high standing. Such has not however always been the case: during the sixteenth century, for instance, it became the practice for Fellows to resign their Fellowships corruptly, selling them in advance for large sums of money to other aspirants. As today, the Fellows have always pursued outside careers, with such famous names as Sir Christopher Wren standing high among the list of eminent men who have been members of this most exclusive of all colleges over the centuries. He became a Fellow at the time of the Commonwealth and was later appointed Savilian Professor of Astronomy. Oliver Cromwell, incidentally, stayed here over the period 1651-1658 when he was the college's Chancellor.

The colleges of Oxford and Cambridge are all places of higher learning, but among the numerous public schools of England there are also to be found many ancient and historically interesting establishments. **Eton College** is probably the best known of all, dating from the year 1440 when Henry VI issued a charter for its foundation, laying the foundation stone for the chapel himself the following year. The oldest surviving part of the school, apart from the chapel, dates from the fifteenth century, and what is called the Upper School was completed in 1694; opposite it, on the eastern side of the yard, is Lupton's Tower, built at the beginning of the sixteenth century. The Old Hall, gained by way of a flight of stairs leading off the cloisters, dates from approximately the year 1450, being a part of Henry VI's original plan.

Eton has not of course failed to keep up with the times, either in the addition of new buildings or in the improvement in methods of education; but from an historic point of view the two factors most readily associated with it are the antiquity and especial fineness of its buildings and the great measure of fame achieved by so many of its pupils over the centuries, men that range from great Prime Ministers like Gladstone, to diplomats and generals and even to poets like Percy Bysshe Shelley.

This is Eton's great achievement, bred admittedly of a certain exclusiveness, but also nurtured by the fine atmosphere of its buildings, of its marvellous old library and a tradition that stems back more than 500 years. Eton has not however always been the most comfortable place for students, many of whom had low opinions of the place, including Gladstone, who described it as 'the greatest pagan school in Christendom'. Living conditions during the college's earlier years were frequently abominable, and there have been many stories passed down about the atrociousness of the food, not to mention the violence of pupil to pupil. It was not until the middle of the nineteenth century that a public outcry necessitated some kind of reform. Until then

there had been several aspects of Eton life that would not perhaps ordinarily be thought of in connection with an educational establishment: noblemen, for instance, were not obliged to have a college tutor and could if they so wished bring their own with them; they also had the privilege of living outside the college, many of them in considerable luxury.

One final educational establishment that deserves to be included here, and that makes a fitting conclusion to this survey, is the **Royal Naval College, Greenwich,** only comparatively recently given its new lease of life as a college of higher education for already commissioned naval officers. The date of this changeover was actually 1873, the building having been acquired by Act of Parliament, but its history stems back a good many years earlier than that.

An extremely long range of grey stone buildings, the college from its Thames-side emin-

Eton College, Lupton's Tower

Royal Naval College, Greenwich

ence stands on the site of an old Royal palace lived in by members of the Royal Family from the early part of the fifteenth century until the time of Charles I. Both Henry VIII and Elizabeth I were born here, and the young Edward VI died here. During the Cromwellian era it naturally passed out of Royal hands, but it came back to them at the restoration, and Charles II immediately initiated a rebuilding programme. He completed only a part of the west wing, now known as the King Charles Wing.

With the accession of William and Mary, at the particular request of Queen Mary, the building underwent the process of conversion into a hospital for superannuated seamen, and this it remained until the hospital was closed by Parliament and handed over to the Admiralty.

The college is of the highest order architecturally, and includes much fine work by Wren, including the Painted Hall situated under one of the twin domes, with paintings by Thornhill. Beneath the other dome is a chapel, also conceived by Wren but rebuilt by James Stuart following closely the external designs of his predecessor. Both are fine additions to this large complex, comprising basically four main blocks.

64